F Is for Firefighting

F Is for Firefighting

By Dori Hillestad Butler   Illustrated by Joan C. Waites

PELICAN PUBLISHING COMPANY
GRETNA 2007

For my father-in-law, Dick, who showed me that
firefighting is more than just a job
—D. H. B.

Library of Congress Cataloging-in-Publication Data

Butler, Dori Hillestad.
 F is for firefighting / by Dori Hillestad Butler ; illustrated by Joan
C. Waites.
     p. cm.
 ISBN-13: 978-1-58980-420-3 (hardcover : alk. paper)
 1. Fire extinction—Juvenile literature. 2. Alphabet books—Juvenile
literature. I. Waites, Joan C., ill. II. Title.
 TH9148.B852 2007
 628.9'2—dc22
                                        2006031113

Printed in China
Published by Pelican Publishing Company, Inc.
1000 Burmaster Street, Gretna, Louisiana 70053

A is for Alarm. Bzzz! Bzzz! The alarm sounds at the fire-house. Someone has dialed 911 and reported a house fire. Firefighters race to their trucks and hurry to the fire.

B is for Bucket Brigade. During the 1700s, there were no fire trucks.

Instead, every home had a leather bucket. When there was a fire, people lined up and passed buckets of water down the "bucket brigade" to put out the fire.

C is for Crash Rescue Vehicle. A crash rescue vehicle is parked at the airport rather than the firehouse. It's built to drive fast and stop fast even though it carries a heavy load of water and foam.

D is for Dalmatian. The Dalmatian is the firehouse mascot. During the 1800s, fire engines were pulled by horses. The firehouse dog ran alongside the horses and scared away other animals or people that might distract the horses on the way to the fire. He also guarded the horses and the fire engine while the firefighters put out the fire.

E is for Equipment. Firefighters carry 80 to 100 pounds of firefighting equipment and rescue gear. Their uniforms weigh around 14 pounds. Their air tanks and face masks weigh around 27 pounds. Firefighters also carry hoses, nozzles, fire extinguishers, ladders, axes, chainsaws, and first-aid supplies.

F is for Firehouse. The firehouse has a dispatcher's center, classrooms, offices, and living quarters for the firefighters. In between calls, firefighters eat, clean house, exercise, train, relax, and even sleep at the firehouse.

G is for Grass Truck. A grass truck is a four-wheel-drive truck that can travel over bumpy ground to reach a fire that is off the road. It carries its own water tank, pump, and miscellaneous firefighting equipment.

H is for Hydrant. In many cities, fire hydrants are color coded so that firefighters know how big the underground water line is. For instance, red hydrants may have small lines, yellow hydrants medium-sized lines, and green hydrants larger lines.

I is for Intersection Control Device. The intersection control device is a white strobe light that's mounted on the top of some fire trucks. It overrides traffic signals so that the fire truck always has a green light.

J is for Jaws of Life®. Many fire trucks carry the Hurst Forcible entry tool, or "Jaws of Life." This machine can cut almost anything. It's most often used to cut apart wrecked vehicles after a car accident so that rescue workers can get to the people who are hurt.

K is for Key Box. Many buildings have key boxes that contain keys to the building. Firefighters have special keys to unlock these boxes so they can get inside the building without breaking the windows.

L is for Ladder Truck. The aerial ladder truck is the largest truck at the firehouse. Most aerial ladders extend 100 feet—high enough to reach the eighth floor of a building. But some can extend as high as 200 feet.

M is for Mobile Command Vehicle. When there is a large fire or disaster and several fire departments are sent to the scene, a mobile command vehicle becomes the fire chiefs' headquarters. Fire chiefs from different fire departments work together inside the vehicle.

N is for nozzle. Fire-hose nozzles come in all different sizes and shapes. Each one sprays the water differently. Some spray a light mist. Others spray a heavy stream. Different fires require different nozzles.

O is for Outrigger. Outriggers are steel legs that hold a heavy truck steady when the ladder is up. Without them, the weight of the ladder could make the truck fall over.

P is for Pumper Truck. The pumper truck is usually the first truck to reach the fire. It holds 500 to 1,000 gallons of water. Firefighters attach hoses to the truck and to nearby fire hydrants. Then they pump water through the truck onto the fire.

Q is for Quint Truck. A quint truck is a combination pumper/ladder truck. "Quint" means "five," and this truck has five essential items on it: a water tank, pump, hose, aerial ladder, and ground ladders. There is also a compartment for rescue equipment. It's a modern, all-purpose fire truck.

R is for Radio. Firefighters use two-way radios to communicate during a fire. The commander gives directions over the radio. Firefighters also carry radios when they are away from the fire station.

S is for Siren. The siren on an emergency vehicle is extra loud to get your attention.

Some sirens are motor-powered. Others are electronic. Motor sirens can only play one sound, but electronic sirens can play five to six different sounds.

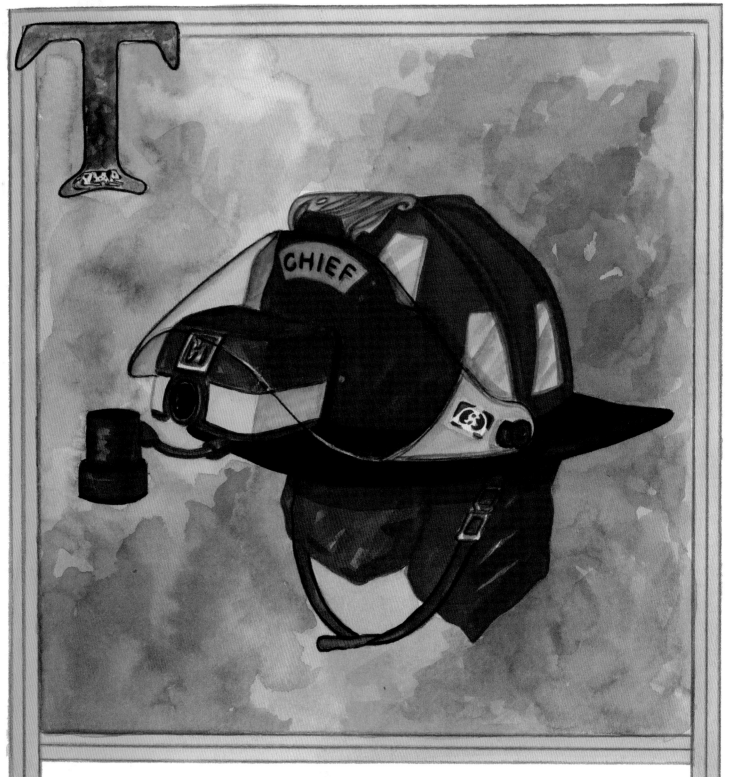

T is for Thermal Imaging Camera. A thermal imaging camera is a special camera that may be mounted on a firefighter's helmet. It allows him to see through dark clouds of smoke so he doesn't trip when he walks into a smoky room. He can also see people and pets who may need rescuing.

U is for Utility Truck. A utility truck is a small truck that carries a variety of supplies including a ladder, extinguisher, first-aid kit, air tanks, lights, camera, and rescue tools. This truck carries everything that the other trucks can't carry. Firefighters can use the utility truck for almost any emergency except putting out a fire.

V is for Variety. Firefighters have a variety of jobs. Besides putting out fires, they help clean up after storms and other disasters. They rescue people who are trapped. They also inspect new buildings and teach people about fire safety.

W is for Water Rescue Vehicle. People who work on water rescue vehicles are trained as firefighters, paramedics, and scuba divers. They help people who are trapped in the water. They also use inflatable lift bags to bring things like bicycles or cars up from the bottom of a lake.

X is for eXtinguisher. Firefighters carry several different fire extinguishers so they can put out different kinds of fires. Firefighters use water on paper or wood fires. They use dry chemicals on oil or gas fires. And they use carbon dioxide on electrical fires.

Y is for Youth Education. Firefighters often visit schools and daycare centers to talk to children about fire safety. Practicing fire safety saves lives.

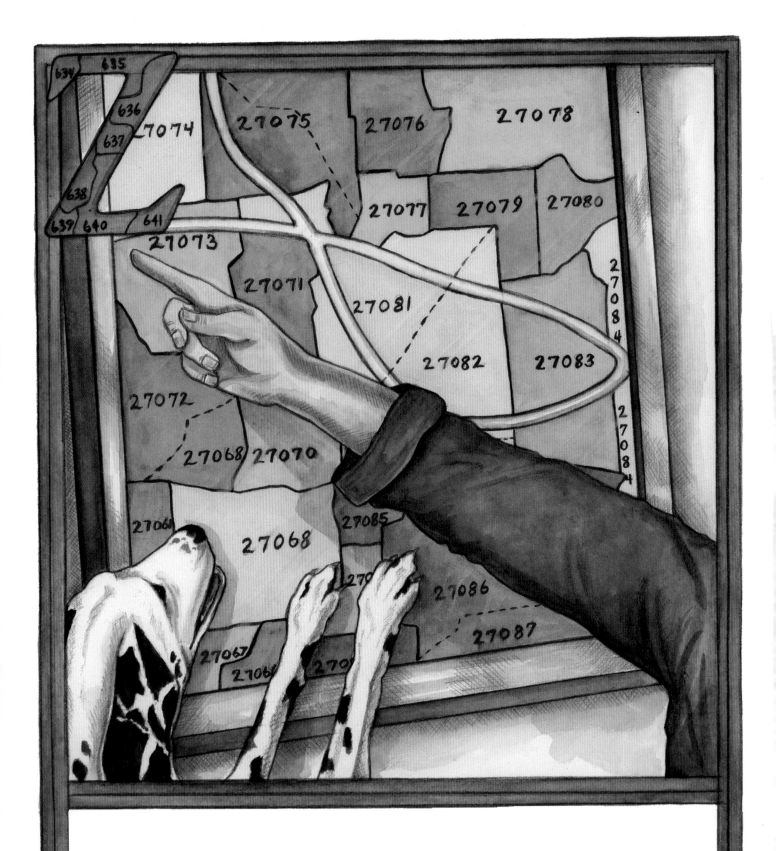

Z is for Zones. Cities are divided into zones. There is one fire station in each zone so firefighters can reach any fire in the city in just a few minutes.